Dawson's Creek

Dawson's Creek

Lisa Degnen

MetroBooks

MetroBooks

An Imprint of Friedman/Fairfax Publishers

©1999 by Michael Friedman Publishing Group, Inc.

Library of Congress Cataloging-in-Publication Data available upon request.

ISBN 1-56799-845-3

Editor: Emily Zelner
Art Director: Kevin Ullrich
Designer: Andrea Karman
Photography Editor: Valerie E. Kennedy

Printed in the U.K. by Butler & Tanner Ltd.

10 9 8 7 6 5 4 3 2 1

For bulk purchases and special sales, please contact:
Friedman/Fairfax Publishers
Attention: Sales Department
15 West 26th Street
New York, NY 10010
212/685-6610
FAX 212/685-1307

Visit our website:
http://www.metrobooks.com

PHOTOGRAPHY CREDITS

AP Photo/Karen Tam: pp. 59, 65, 71

Archive Photos: pp. 17, 69, 79

Everett Collection: pp. 8-9 all, 50, 57, 70, 84, 88, 91

Globe Photos, Inc.: pp. 14, 38, 55, 64, 73, 83, 89; ©Fitzroy Barrett: pp. 20, 22, 27, 86; ©Lisa Rose: p. 23, 30, 95; ©Milan Ryba: p. 21

Globe Photos, Inc./Rangefinders: p. 34

Kobal Collection: ©Guy D'Alema: p. 11; ©Andrew Eccles: pp. 6 top, 61; ©Frank Ockenfels: p. 60, 67

London Features International: ©Kevin Cummins: p. 42 top left; ©Anthony Cutajar: p. 46; ©Barbra Deliman/NGI: pp. 5, 48-49; ©David Hum: p. 42 top right; ©Gary Merrin: p. 47; ©Kevin Mazur: p. 43, 44

The Neal Peters Collection: pp. 18, 19

Photofest: pp. 6 bottom, 7 both, 12-13, 25, 26, 28, 29, 31, 35, 36, 39, 40, 41, 52-53 all, 54, 58, 74-75, 80, 82, 87, 93

Retna Limited, U.S.A.: ©Bob Berg: p. 42 bottom right-43; ©Jay Blakesberg: p. 42 bottom left, 45; ©Joseph Marzullo: pp. 16, 62; ©Walter McBride: p. 76; ©Barry Talesnick: p. 32

Contents

Introduction

Addicted to *Dawson's Creek*? Help is on the way. An insider's look at the show, including detailed profiles of the four young stars that have made *Dawson's Creek* a sizzling hit and an in-depth treatment of the show's first season that lay the foundation for this teen drama, is at your fingertips. Check out the original episode titles, which get their names from the movies, and are among the many references to pop culture on *Dawson's Creek*. The episodes were renamed after the completion of the first season, but you can find the real thing here.

The show is set in a picture-perfect Boston suburb. But though the picture may look flawless, the four lead characters have anything but perfect lives. Each episode details the kinds of trials and turmoil that every teen must deal with growing up. Dawson Leery is the great-looking guy who dreams of being the next Steven Spielberg. He is as passionate about movies as he is about his friends. Dawson's best friend is Josephine "Joey" Potter, a teenage tomboy who is slowly blossoming into a beautiful woman. Coming from a dysfunctional family, Joey has her own problems, and is confused over her emerging feelings toward Dawson. Pacey Witter is Dawson's other childhood pal. He's a wisecracking guy who tends to find himself in situations that are usually way over his head.

FROM LEFT TO RIGHT

The kiss that everyone wanted to see. On the first season-ending cliff hanger, Dawson finally realizes that Joey is the girl of his dreams.

Pacey and his teacher Tamara's romance certainly got people talking. Tamara is played by Leann Hunley, former star of the soap opera *Days of Our Lives*.

When Jen decides she really does want a relationship with Dawson, he's already started to dream of Joey.

By the time the gang's sophomore year has begun, a new girl—the blond and beautiful Jennifer Lindley—arrives as Dawson's next-door neighbor. She may live next door, but Jen certainly isn't typical. She has moved from New York with an entire set of problems—and secrets—of her own.

Together they explore new boundaries that will test themselves and their friendships.

"We wanted our kids to be really articulate and very good at expressing themselves, while they deal with the same problems and sense of confusion that other teens are dealing with," says Paul Stupin, one of the show's executive producers.

The great writing and the talented teen actors have made the show a hit. Nearly two million teens tune in every week—and that's not counting all the fans who set their VCRs!

Despite its success, the show hasn't been without its controversial moments. The greatest criticism of *Dawson's Creek* has been about its portrayal of teacher Tamara falling for Pacey, who happens to be one of her students. Critics have said that this is "destructive psychologically," and that a sexual relationship between a teacher and a student is inappropriate subject matter for a teenage audience. They say that even though the relationship ends badly, the show did not do enough to demonstrate that it was wrong.

However, the WB network, which airs the show in the United States, says it has acted responsibly and that, as usual, adults underestimate the intelligence of teenagers.

"Do I feel we've acted responsibly? Absolutely," says WB chief Jamie Kellner. "I don't think there's anything in this program we haven't seen in the news or in the movies, and we feel we did it in a responsible way."

In fact, most teens say they like the show because it does reflect real life, and even though the cast and crew believe they deal with issues responsibly, they are never going to try and give you a lesson in morality.

"There's nothing preachy about it," says the show's creator, Kevin Williamson. "The moment anyone says anything that sounds like a message, the characters discard it. They say, 'So what did we learn from this *90210* moment?'"

The cast on the waterfront in Wilmington, North Carolina, where the show is filmed. The group is now recognized everywhere they go in the historic southern town and their pictures are on the wall of the local coffee shop. The show uses the same set that was once used to film the TV show *Matlock.*

The Players

Meet the bright young stars of *Dawson's Creek*. Go behind the scenes with Michelle Williams, James Van Der Beek, Katie Holmes, and Joshua Jackson—find out who they are, where they come from, and how they got to *Dawson's Creek!*

Dawson's Creek is really the first starring role for James, but it certainly won't be his last. He did appear in the 1995 movie *Angus* and got his first up-close look at teen idolatry when he acted alongside Claire Danes in *I Love You, I Love You Not*.

On the show, Dawson seems fairly unaware that his good looks turn girls' heads, but in real life James must know by now that he's a looker. *People* magazine recently named him one of their "50 Most Beautiful People."

"James is so good-looking, yet he has this incredible analytical, intelligent side," says Kevin Williamson. "James is very much Dawson—a couple of years down the road."

Costar Michelle Williams agrees. "James is very graceful and unassuming," she explains. "A very smooth, even, cool guy."

Aside from all that stuff about looks, James says the greatest praise he ever got was when his agent said he reminded him of the great actor Jimmy Stewart.

James says that he can really identify with the character of Dawson. "I think a lot of the things that he goes through are pretty universal," he says. "I relate to him very well. We're both naive, a bit innocent and very impassioned at a young age.

James is taking a break from his college classes at New Jersey's Drew University while he works on the show. He says he has always been consumed with the desire to act.

"The cool thing about Dawson is his intentions are never anything but honorable. He makes mistakes out of ignorance or lack of experience as opposed to malice, which is nice."

James was raised in the small town of Cheshire, Connecticut. He is the oldest of three children. His dad, Jim, is an account manager for Southern New England Telecommunications Corp., and his mom, Melinda, is a gymnastics studio owner.

James was a high school football star until he got a concussion in eighth grade. Then he turned his attention to acting. His first

ABOVE

James' winning looks, depth of character, and talent for acting have made him the hot young star that he is today.

OPPOSITE

James has said in interviews that he has a lot in common with the character he plays on TV. This probably accounts, in part, for his spectacular portrayal of Dawson Leery—the other part, of course, is his gift for doing what he loves most, acting.

big role was playing Danny Zuko in a school production of *Grease*. "They dyed my hair black," he laughs.

By the age of sixteen, James had really been bitten by the acting bug and decided to pursue a career. He landed an agent right away, but the work came more slowly.

ABOVE

James is impressed with the authenticity of *Dawson's Creek*. He says, "The dialogue isn't necessarily representative of the way every kid speaks, but it's absolutely representative of the way every kid feels."

OPPOSITE

James is very modest about his reputation as a heartthrob. "I honestly don't see how someone could get a big ego out of it, because it's not you," says James.

ABOVE

James Van Der Beek and Michelle Williams at a celebrity softball event. "James is very graceful and unassuming," says Michelle, "a very smooth, even, cool guy."

OPPOSITE

James loves receiving fan mail—and there's plenty of it! He says that he tries to read and respond to every letter he gets. It just goes to show that James is indeed as sensitive as the character he portrays on TV.

"My mother saw my intense interest and said, 'If this is something you really want to try, I'll take you to New York for the summer.'" Before college he managed to land a role in the off-Broadway play *Finding the Sun*.

He was an English major on the dean's list at New Jersey's Drew University—until he started to land more and more acting parts. He's now on temporary leave from the university.

While he is quickly becoming a household name, most fans don't realize that James very nearly blew his audition for *Dawson's Creek*.

"He was really nervous and it showed," says Kevin Williamson, who gave James a quick pep talk at the audition. "He came back into the room and stunned us. We knew he was Dawson. He's very bright, but he's also very vulnerable. I like that because it keeps him fifteen years old."

Life has certainly changed for James, but he's trying hard to stay true to his hometown roots. "I've met some cool people in L.A. They took me around and showed me the whole Hollywood scene," he says. "I saw people wearing sunglasses at night! I always thought that was a joke, but they really do it!"

ABOVE

James Van Der Beek and Katie Holmes take a break from acting to work on publicity for *Dawson's Creek*.

OPPOSITE

"He's the good-looking, polite, college-educated kid who says 'sir' and 'ma'am,'" says Joshua Jackson about fellow actor, James Van Der Beek.

Katie Holmes never dreamed she would one day be famous while she was growing up in Toledo, Ohio, but she is certainly ecstatic now that she's practically a household name. She admits that she still gets a certain thrill seeing herself on the small screen every Wednesday night. "The others will all probably say, 'Oh no, I won't watch.' But I'll admit that I'll be watching thinking, 'Oh my God! I thought they were going to use a different shot,'" she laughs.

Katie started acting in theater productions in high school. While attending a national modeling and talent convention in New York City, she met a talent manager who convinced her to come to Los Angeles to try out for a number of pilots. In her very first audition she absolutely swept away the casting director when she tried out for *The Ice Storm*, starring Sigourney Weaver and Kevin Kline. She got the part and some great reviews.

During her senior year in high school she played Lola in her high school production of *Damn Yankees*. She sent a videotape of that performance for the *Dawson's Creek* audition. The producers wanted her to fly out immediately for another audition, but it conflicted with the run of her high school production. Instead of bowing out on her classmates, Katie said she couldn't go to Los Angeles for the call back. Fortunately fate intervened and the *Dawson's Creek* producers rescheduled her audition. She landed the role of Joey.

Katie prefers a natural to a made-up look. So even when she wears makeup, she likes to keep it light. This works out well when she plays tomboy Joey on *Dawson's Creek*.

ABOVE

Katie Holmes was just a high school junior when she won a role in the hit movie *The Ice Storm*. Since then her acting career has skyrocketed and her starring role on *Dawson's Creek* certainly has given her some hot exposure.

OPPOSITE

"Joey," says Katie Holmes, "is the girl who usually doesn't get the guy." But by the end of the first season, it looked like Joey had won the man of her dreams.

Joey, of course, is a tormented teen who has had a rough time not only with her family but also with her love life. Katie says she understands why Joey can be merciless with her put-downs to Jen, like, "I love your hair color—what number is it?"

Joey has lost her mother to cancer, her dad's in prison, and she's hopelessly in love with Dawson. "Joey has to come back with her wit. It's the only way she knows how to deal with her pathetic existence," Katie explains. "Only a few girls get to be prom queens and get all the guys. Those girls are like Jen. Joey isn't the girl who gets all the guys. I wasn't like that either, so I can relate."

ABOVE

James Marsden stars with Katie Holmes in the movie *Disturbing Behavior*.

"Success is about getting an education and being happy," Katie says.

OPPOSITE

Katie in *Disturbing Behavior*. Katie loves acting but she never thought she could

make it. "I wanted to be an actress," she says, "but I'm from Ohio. I told myself to

get a grip." Boy, was she wrong.

Katie might not think she's a great beauty, but every guy who sees her thinks differently. "You could take a picture of her in the dark and she'd look good," says costar Josh Jackson.

Katie says the biggest difference between her and Joey is that "at fifteen, I wasn't that concerned with sex. I come from a small town, so I'm very sheltered. Basically, I was concerned with family, friends, and high school plays. My concerns are now career and college, but still family and friends are very important."

Katie says that, like Joey, she too was once in love with her best friend. "It was painful," she remembers.

Katie lives in Wilmington, North Carolina nearby the other cast members when she is filming the show.

ABOVE

Katie with her real-life mom, Kathleen, and her sister Hope at this year's

Kids Choice Awards.

OPPOSITE

Katie has not forgotten her hometown roots and her hometown of Toledo, Ohio has

certainly not forgotten her. Mark Tooman of Toledo's chamber of commerce

has remarked, "She is, I think, the all-American young lady. Somebody that

you can be proud to say is from your hometown."

JOSHUA JACKSON

ALSO KNOWN AS
PACEY WITTER

BIRTHDATE:
JUNE 11, 1978

Josh is a very different guy from the wild and crazy Pacey. "Of course there is an obvious difference," Josh says. "He's fictional and I'm real."

Well, at least they are alike in the wisecracking department. "I have always been a jokester," Josh admits. "I inherited from my mother a terribly sarcastic sense of humor. The characters I've played have always been good guys. Finally I get to be the wiseass."

Josh, who likes to read philosophy books in his spare time, is the old pro of the cast. He has starred in all three of Disney's *Mighty Ducks* movies and has had roles on lots of TV shows, including *MacGyver, Champs,* and *The Outer Limits.*

Josh grew up in Vancouver, British Columbia, and landed his first acting role when he was just nine years old, in a commercial for the British Columbia tourism board.

The six-foot-tall Canadian says that from the time he first saw himself onscreen he knew that acting was something he wanted to pursue.

The one thing everyone wants to know about Josh is whether or not he has ever fallen for an older woman like his character has. "I've only dated someone about one or two years older than me," he says. "But I've had lots of crushes on older women, so I've had a vast amount of fantasy experiences."

"I don't know what I'd do if I didn't act," says Joshua Jackson. "It lets my feelings show. And that's why I love it."

ABOVE

Joshua Jackson starred in all three *Mighty Ducks* movies for Disney. He says moving from the PG movies to a controversial role as a student who seduces his teacher on *Dawson's Creek* has changed his image back home in Vancouver. "I called them up and said, 'Man, you'll never believe what I get to do on this show!'" he laughs.

OPPOSITE

Joshua Jackson admits that he had an awkward phase when he was in high school. "It was the exact same thing," he says. "We were all thinking about sex, like that was a huge deal. We had to start learning how to deal with the other gender."

MICHELLE WILLIAMS

ALSO KNOWN AS
JENNIFER LINDLEY

BIRTHDATE:
September 9, 1980

Born in Kalispell, Montana, Michelle eventually moved with her family to San Diego, California, when she was nine years old. Michelle says people tell her she looks like Jewel. She remembers her own high school years as complete hell. "If there were good times, I don't remember them," she says. "I had no friends and no one to talk to! I spent every lunch in the bathroom, hiding in the stall. It's weird to be back at school on the set, opening lockers and stuff.

"I just hated the people, the atmosphere, and the catty fights between girls. The girls just didn't understand that there was life past clothes, makeup, and boys. . . . I left after my freshman year. I was home-schooled for another year until I graduated early.

"When I visit my parents, I sometimes have to go pick up my sister Paige, who's at the same school now. When I see the girls I went to school with I still get the shakes and my stomach hurts."

Life has certainly improved for Michelle. When she turned sixteen she moved away from home to Los Angeles—alone—to work on her acting career. "I know it's crazy," she says. "My mother was scared out of her mind." The gamble paid off for Michelle, who landed roles in the movies *Lassie* and *A Thousand Acres,* the latter with Michelle Pfeiffer.

Michelle is as stylish and sophisticated looking off the set of *Dawson's Creek* as she is on. She prefers a feminine and mature look, but she says that most importantly she likes to feel comfortable in her clothing.

ABOVE

One of Michelle's first roles was in *Lassie* with Thomas Guiry. Michelle has also done guest spots on *Home Improvement* and *Step By Step.*

OPPOSITE

Michelle says that she is sometimes very much like her character Jennifer Lindley. "We're both old souls in the sense that we grew up fast and experienced a lot of things at an early age."

Now she loves her life on *Dawson's Creek* and spends her free time on the beach in Wilmington with Katie Holmes. "I wish I could have expressed my feelings like Jen does," Michelle says of her TV counterpart. She does say that she and Jen are very different when it comes to their views of the opposite sex. "I can't really tap into Jen's sex concerns," Michelle says. "My concerns at that age were staying on track and making it in whatever career I'd chosen."

These days Michelle says she eats, sleeps, and breathes acting. "It's been a while since I've been on a date," she explains. "I barely have enough time to sleep. It's been so crazy. Not that it wouldn't be nice to not be alone all the time."

ABOVE

Adam Hann-Byrd, Jodi Lynn O'Keefe, Josh Hartnett, and Michelle Williams in

Halloween H20.

OPPOSITE

Josh Hartnett and Michelle Williams get frightened in Halloween H20.

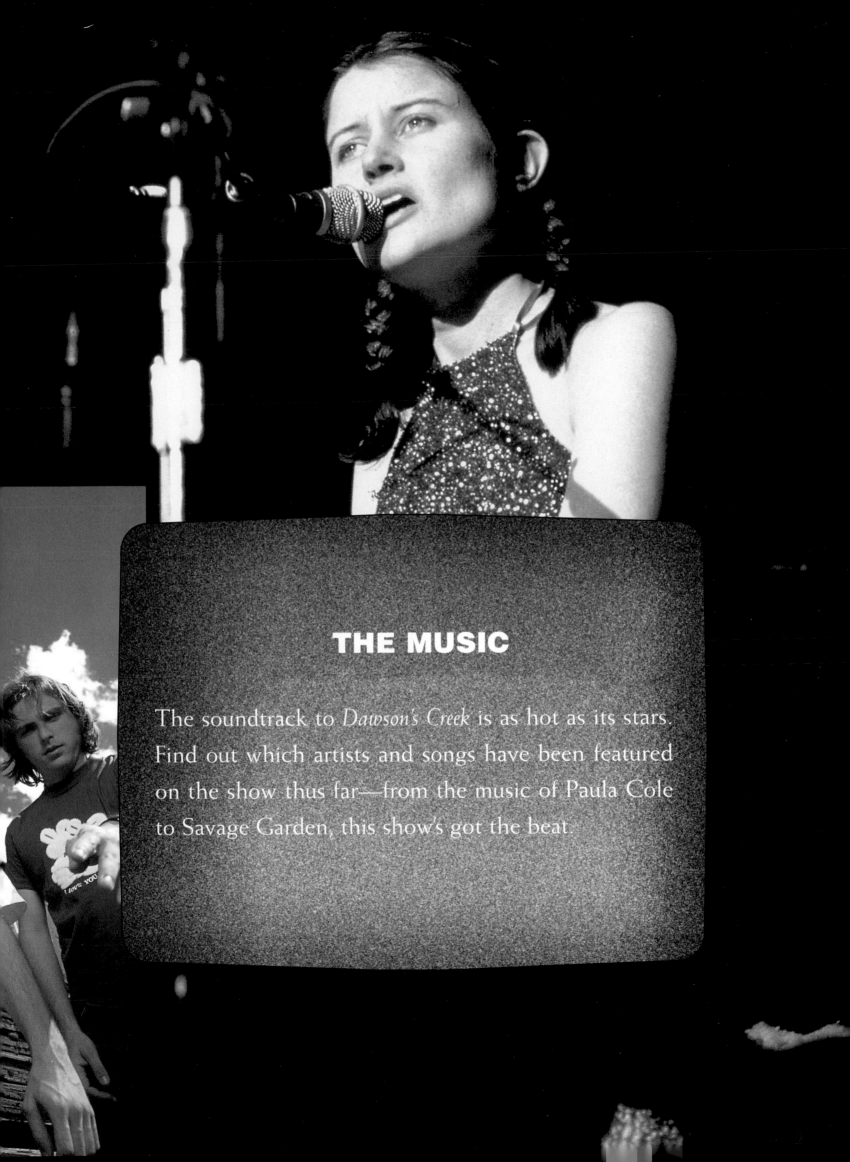

THE MUSIC

The soundtrack to *Dawson's Creek* is as hot as its stars. Find out which artists and songs have been featured on the show thus far—from the music of Paula Cole to Savage Garden, this show's got the beat.

The tunes that accompany *Dawson's Creek* have had a lot to do with the show's success. The music is as hip and interesting as the show's four young stars.

But did you know that the show's theme was supposed to be a completely different song?

At first, Alanis Morrisette's song "Hand In My Pocket" was set to be the theme and advance tapes of the pilot episode even had the well-known song on it. But it seems that Alanis had a change of heart, saying that she didn't want her song to be known as a TV tune.

Paula Cole was only too happy to step in with her hit "I Don't Want to Wait."

"At first I was reluctant," Paula says, "but when I saw the show, I believed in it."

Creator Kevin Williamson thinks the Paula Cole tune has turned out perfectly. "The show is about the constantly changing feelings of teenagers, and you can feel the full range of emotions in her music."

Here are highlights from the soundtrack that has rocked the world of *Dawson's Creek*:

"EMOTIONS IN MOTION"

The BoDeans, "Hey Pretty Girl"

Sophie B. Hawkins, "As I Lay Me Down"

Chumbawamba, "Tubthumping"

Say-So, "Mercy Me"

Jann Arden, "Good Mother"

The Pretenders, "I'll Stand by You"

"DIRTY DANCING"

Nowhere Blossoms, "Am I Cool"

Sarah Masen, "Flames of Truth"

Savage Garden, "I Want You"

Abra Moore, "Happiness"

Peer, "Ooh, Ahh... Just a Little Bit"

Paul Chiten, "Pretty Strange"

The Autumns, "Apple"

Paul Chiten, "But You"

Jann Arden, "You Don't Know Me"

"PRELUDE TO A KISS"

Billie Myers, "First Time"

Wake, "Too Many Times"

Eddi Reader, "The Right Place"

Tanya Donelly, "Pretty Deep"

The Slugs, "Kingdom"

Toad the Wet Sprocket, "All I Want"

Sophie Zelmani, "I'll Remember You"

Meredith Brooks, "What Would Happen"

"CARNAL KNOWLEDGE"

Kyf Brewer, "Beautiful Thing"

Hang Ups, "Top of the Morning"

Barenaked Ladies, "I Know"

Toad the Wet Sprocket, "Amnesia"

Devlins, "World Outside"

Tom Snow, "That's What Love Can Do"

Sarah McLachlan, "Full of Grace"

Say-So, "Stand By Me"

ABOVE
Named after a sketch by the Monty Python troupe, Toad the Wet Sprocket was one of the hottest alternative rock bands of the early '90s.

OPPOSITE
Singer and songwriter Paula Cole received her first big break in 1992 when she was invited to perform on Peter Gabriel's world tour and it was not long before her songs hit the tops of the charts. Cole won the Grammy for Best New Artist in 1998.

"BLOWN AWAY"

R.E.M., "It's the End of the World as We
  Know It"

Mark Cohn, "Healing Hands"

"LOOK WHO'S TALKING"

Amanda Marshall, "Sittin' on Top of the
  World"

Andrew Dorff, "Insecuriosity"

Susanna Hoffs, "All I Want"

Beth Neilsen, "Seven Shades of Blue"

"IN THE COMPANY OF MEN"

Savage Garden, "Truly, Madly, Deeply"

Days of the New, "Touch, Peel and Stand"

Space Monkeys, "We Are the Supercool"

Super Deluxe, "Your Pleasure is Mine"

The Slugs, "Requiem for a Light Weight"

Nowhere Blossoms, "I'm Not Sleeping"

Judge Nothing, "Nashville"

Sounder, "I Don't Want to Feel"

Judge Nothing, "Monkey Mind"

Swerve, "Right Today"

Ron Sexsmith, "Thinking Out Loud"

"PRETTY WOMAN"

Eve, "Small Town Trap"

Susan Sandberg, "Girl With All the Good Boys"

Chicken Pox, "Pretty Face"

Amanda Marshall, "Fall From Grace"

Goldfinger, "Superman"

Boublil, "On My Own"

Chantal Kreviazuk, "Surrounded"

"BREAKING AWAY"

Dog's Eye View, "What Do You Do?"

Sarah McLachlan, "Angel"

Edwin McCain, "I'll Be"

Melodie Crittenden, "Broken Road"

Beth Neilsen Chapman, "Say Goodnight"

"THE KISS"

Beth Nielsen Chapman, "Say Goodnight"

Fastball, "Out of My Head"

Heather Nova, "London Rain"

John Hiatt, "Have a Little Faith in Me"

Smashing Pumpkins, "Perfect"

"ALTERNATIVE LIFESTYLES"

Harvey Danger, "Flagpole Sitta"

Catie Curtis, "The Party's Over"

Newsboys, "WooHoo"

Paula Cole, "I Don't Want to Wait"

"TAMARA'S RETURN"

Donna Lewis, "Harvest Moon"

Tori Amos, "Northern Lad"

Shawn Mullins, "And on a Rainy Night"

Seven Mary Three, "Each Little Mystery"

"THE DANCE"

Kenny Loggins, "Footloose"

Sixpence None the Richer, "Kiss Me"

Reel Big Fish, "Sell Out"

Garbage, "Special"

Donna Lewis, "Take Me Home"

Wine Field, "Man on a Mast"

ABOVE

Darren Hayes and Daniel Jones, the Savage Garden duo, have set countless hearts on fire with their love ballad titled "Truly, Madly, Deeply"—the hit song was featured on the episode, "In the Company of Men."

OPPOSITE

Andrew Dorff's quirky pop sensibilities enliven the *Dawson's Creek* soundtrack.

The Episodes

The first season of *Dawson's Creek* introduced us to Dawson and his gang—their histories, hopes, and dreams. And the events of the first season lay the foundation for the developments to come. If you've ever missed an episode, you'll find this section a handy reference—a window into the past. If you're just tuning in now, here's the essential program guide where you can find out what you need to know to understand the latest season.

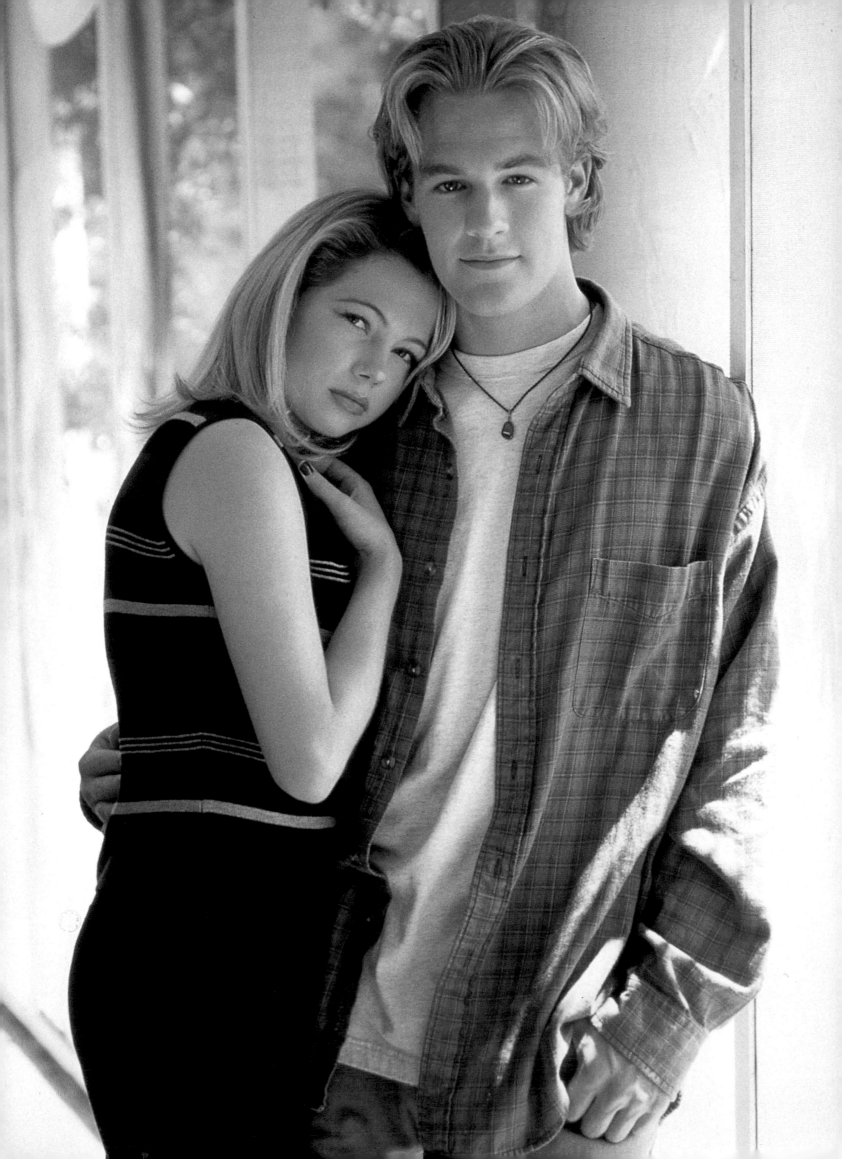

EPISODE

1

"EMOTIONS IN MOTION"

The show's very first episode opens with good-looking fifteen-year-old Dawson Leery talking to his pal Josephine "Joey" Potter about his dream of being the next Steven Spielberg.

It's summer and Joey and Dawson are spending a night together—just like they've always done. Joey says that now that they are older, maybe they shouldn't share a bed.

But Dawson tells Joey they are practically brother and sister and they would never let sexual tension get in the way of their friendship. Since Joey's mom has died of cancer and her father is in prison, Dawson and her sister, Bessie, are the only family she has. So she decides he is right and she'll spend the night.

Meanwhile, beautiful New Yorker Jennifer Lindley moves next door to the Leery family. She has moved to Capeside to help her grandmother take care of her sick grandfather. Whatever happened in New York has apparently made Jen reject all forms of religion, which immediately causes problems with her church-going grandmother.

Dawson and his best bud Pacey Witter are taken with her beauty, but it looks like Dawson is just a bit more taken with her than Pacey. He is spotted chatting with her on the dock and showing

Dawson's obsession with Jennifer Lindley preoccupied most of the first season. The beautiful blonde moved from New York to Capeside to live with her grandparents and Dawson immediately fell head over heels.

her the "studio," which also happens to be his bedroom. For the first time, Joey feels pangs of jealousy when she sees her old pal and the pretty blonde talking.

Pacey is working at a video store when a beautiful older woman walks in and asks him for a copy of *The Graduate*. She flirts with him and Pacey happily flirts back. Even when he finds out that she is going to be one of his teachers at Capeside High, he still is determined to carry on the flirtation. In fact, he is so determined to chase after his new teacher that he convinces Dawson to come with him to the movies so he can run into her. Dawson decides this would be a good opportunity to get to know Jen a little better, so he asks her to come along and also talks an unhappy Joey into going too, so it won't be so awkward.

But the movie turns out to be a night of tension instead of a relaxing evening's entertainment. When Pacey finally finds his tempting teacher, Tamara, he ends up getting punched by Tamara's date, and Joey embarrasses herself by making biting remarks to Jen and Dawson.

Eventually, Pacey runs into Tamara at the marina, where he tells her off, saying that she used him to prove to herself that she's still attractive even though she's an older woman. Tamara plants a passionate kiss on the stunned Pacey and then runs away.

FROM LEFT TO RIGHT

Dawson fell all over Jen when she first came to town from New York and Joey was beside herself with jealousy. "When Jen starts to have that closeness [with Dawson] that Joey does, that's when it starts infringing on what's familiar and old," Michelle explains.

Jen came to Joey's rescue and helped her hatch a great plan against a boy who had told the entire school that he had sex with Joey.

On the show Jen and Joey can't stand each other most of the time, but off camera Michelle and Katie spend a lot of their time hanging out together. "I don't think Joey hates Jen because she's blond or whatever," Michelle says. "It's more because of the relationship Jen begins to develop with Dawson."

Later that night, Dawson and Joey talk about their feelings. They agree that they are both attractive people, but not attracted to each other. But Joey says that they have reached the point where they will be unable to talk to each other about everything. Dawson disagrees. But to show him that she's right, Joey asks Dawson how many times a day he masturbates. He tells her to go to sleep. As she's walking away, Dawson shouts after her that he takes care of his business in the morning, dreaming about Katie Couric.

Just when you thought all was going to end well, Joey spots Dawson's mom kissing another man—confirming the suspicions that she's been having an affair.

ABOVE

When James was younger he thought he might be a professional athlete one day, but a concussion at the age of thirteen prevented him from playing on the school football team that year. Instead he landed a role in his high school's production of *Grease*, and from there he knew he wanted to be an actor.

OPPOSITE

Katie says she was once in love with a friend, just like Joey is in love with Dawson. "I had that experience," she says. "It was painful."

EPISODE 2
"DIRTY DANCING"

In the show's second episode, Dawson is set to direct his big "movie." The first time around, Joey's character is ready to kiss Pacey's character, but since Joey is completely turned off by Pacey, she refuses to kiss him. So Dawson decides to kill off Joey's character and writes a replacement character for Jen. Joey's character runs up and down the dock in a scene where she is killed, soaked in fake blood.

When Jen helps Joey get cleaned up afterward, they get to talk one on one for the first time and, remarkably, they manage to get along.

During the next scene, Jen and Pacey get to act out the big "kiss." But in the middle of the scene, in a moment of jealousy, Dawson yells, "Cut," and says, "It doesn't work."

Dawson later asks his father for some advice about kissing. Dad tells him that it's important for the bottom lip to "dance." He talks about the first time he locked lips with Dawson's mom. She said her lips were a little dry, so he put Chapstick on his own lips and kissed her.

It looks like Pacey will beat Dawson to the punch when it comes to passionate kissing. He has been following teacher Tamara around school, asking her if it's their age difference that's keeping

Pacey takes a walk on the wild side when he romantically pursues his teacher Tamara. In real life, Joshua says he's had lots of crushes on older women, but has only dated girls a year or two older than himself.

them apart. Tamara is trying her best just to ignore Pacey. But once they see each other again at the marina, they have an open conversation and apologize for their respective behavior. The attraction between them, however, just can't be ignored, and they end up in a long, lingering kiss.

Back at school, Dawson is upset to learn that his rival, high school football star Cliff, is planning on making a movie too—about his valiant achievements on the field. And if that weren't bad enough, Cliff is putting the moves on Jen. When Cliff asks Jen to go to the dance with

him, Dawson is out of his head with jealousy.

Dawson finally decides to go to the dance at the last minute and asks Joey to come with him. She agrees, but just before they leave, she has a showdown with Dawson's mom about what she witnessed at the end of the previous episode.

That evening, Dawson tries to cut in on a dance between Jen and Cliff. Before long, he's in the middle of an argument with Cliff, and Jen has walked out.

Later, as Dawson and Joey are walking home and talking about what a disaster the evening has

Michelle Williams says, "Pacey's the guy you fool around with, but Dawson's the one you take home to Mom."

been, Dawson spots Jen. As Dawson rushes to try to make amends with Jen, Joey wishes him well and hopes he gets the kiss he really wants.

Dawson and Jen agree to try and take things slowly and together they have their first slow dance under the stars.

Michelle says it's sometimes a bit weird for her to be playing high school student Jen, because in real life she hated high school so much that she dropped out and was home-schooled. At sixteen she moved alone to Los Angeles to become an actress. "I know it's crazy," she says. "My mother was scared out of her mind."

ABOVE

James says he tries not to think too much about being the star of the show. "There's pressure in that I don't want to let anybody down," he says. "I look at the great work everybody else is doing around me and I don't want to disappoint. But I don't feel like I'm carrying the show."

OPPOSITE

Unlike his school-hating character, Joshua Jackson actually loves learning. In his spare time, this nineteen-year-old likes to read books on philosophy.

EPISODE 3
"PRELUDE TO A KISS"

The episode begins with Dawson and Joey talking about what makes for the perfect kiss. Joey says there's no way to create the perfect kiss. Dawson says he plans on creating the perfect kiss with Jen.

Joey is working at her sister's restaurant when Dawson and Pacey walk in. She sits down with them for a while, then a great-looking guy comes in and catches her eye. They stare at each other for a long time. A spark with someone other than Dawson?

Later Tamara calls Pacey in after school to tell him he's flunking. Pacey says he's deliberately trying to flunk so he can be tutored by a certain beautiful teacher. After Tamara finally becomes his tutor, she promises him rewards if he gets the questions right. When he answers the questions correctly, she tells him to strip. At first, Pacey isn't sure if she's serious, but when she starts to unbutton her blouse he gets the idea. When Pacey becomes visibly uncomfortable, Tamara jokingly asks if it's his first time. When Pacey says it is, Tamara begins to reconsider her offer and says that what they are doing is wrong. But Pacey changes her mind by telling her that he believes two wrongs *do* make a right.

Michelle and James out on the town. James says he doesn't pay any attention to critics who have said that *Dawson's Creek* places too much emphasis on sex. "It's been mainly adults who have the problem," he says. "No one under twenty has said, 'That's too much sex; that's not the way it really is.' "

Back at school, Dawson finds that he has become the slave assistant to annoying producer Nellie. She is making Dawson do all kinds of stupid jobs and when he offers some simple suggestions on how to make the production run more smoothly, she yells at him.

Meanwhile, Joey has found her mystery man, Anderson, a wealthy preppy guy. The new duo spend the next day together sailing, but Joey has told Anderson that she is someone else, because she fears the real Joey could never attract a guy like this.

After a great day together, the two have a great night and Joey gets her first really romantic kiss. She suggests that maybe they could go out again together sometime. Anderson agrees and gives Joey his phone number before leaving, but she accidentally drops it when she pulls away in her car.

In the next scene, Dawson and Jen are up on a mountain in a "No Trespassing Area." Dawson has his camera running in the beautiful spot. Just when he leans in to kiss Jen for the first time, she asks

Dawson makes his move on Jen. Can he create the perfect kiss with her?

why the camera is still running. Dawson explains that it's all part of his plan to create the perfect kiss and admits his obsession with trying to make his life run like a movie.

Suddenly they hear a car pulling up and have to run and hide under a bench. There they kiss for the very first time. The couple that runs past them and behind a tree is Tamara and Pacey, who are caught on Dawson's camera making love.

To make ends meet, Joey works as a waitress at the Ice House restaurant. She lives with her sister and her sister's boyfriend because her dad's in prison for conspiring to sell marijuana and her mom died of cancer.

EPISODE
4
"CARNAL KNOWLEDGE"

While viewing a number of videotapes, Joey and Dawson happen to pop one in the VCR that shows Tamara kissing a man they can't recognize. When they tell Pacey and Jen what they have seen, Pacey laughs but is clearly nervous.

Later, Dawson comes home to find Pacey rummaging through his room looking for the tape. When Dawson gives him the tape, Pacey comes clean and admits that he is the guy on the film.

There's another blow to come for Dawson. When he and Jen go to visit Dawson's mom at the television studio where she works, he accidentally sees his mother kissing her co-anchor. Dawson is devastated. When he tells Joey about what he's seen, he finds out that she already knows all about it and he explodes. He tells Joey that their friendship is now officially over.

Dawson turns to Jen for some sympathy. When they start to talk about their own relationship, Jen tells him that she's not a virgin. He doesn't let Jen know it, but secretly Dawson is shocked.

Pacey has a bout of jealousy when he sees Tamara talking to the film teacher, Mr. Gold, and he tells her she has to choose which guy she wants. Tamara laughs and tells Pacey that the only way that Mr. Gold would be interested in her was if she were a man. Pacey is absolutely stunned that Mr. Gold is gay.

Jen realizes that Dawson is avoiding her. She tells Joey that Dawson is upset because she revealed that she is not a virgin. Joey reassures her that Dawson will come around—eventually. Meanwhile, Dawson is on the verge of telling his dad what he's seen, but at the last minute he chickens out. In the final scene, Joey and Dawson make up and decide their friendship is worth saving.

James and Katie have become close friends off camera. Katie says they are slowly adapting to their new fame. "I can buy nicer things for people," she says. "But it's not like we are going overboard and shopping all the time. I think we have good heads on our shoulders."

EPISODE
5
"BLOWN AWAY"

A hurricane is headed straight for Capeside. But there's also a storm brewing in Dawson's house. Dawson explodes at his mom about her affair, even though his dad is still unaware of what's going on.

Dawson's dad invites Joey, Jen, her grandmother, and others to come to their house to find shelter in the storm. Jen and Joey later talk about how big they think Dawson's manhood is and whether he is carrying a rifle or a pistol.

Pacey and his deputy brother, Doug, put up No Swimming signs on the beach and then head over to Tamara's house to help her board it up. When the three of them start to talk, it becomes clear that Doug is attracted to Tamara. Pacey is infuriated by Doug's flirting and tries to sabotage his brother's overtures by telling Tamara that Doug is gay. When Doug uncovers Pacey's lie he explodes and suddenly pulls his gun on him. At that moment Pacey is forced to confess his lie to Tamara, who is taken aback and horrified by his brother's violent reaction.

Back at Dawson's house, Mrs. Leery has decided to confess her affair to her husband, even though Dawson is in the room. Ironically, the power goes out right after Mrs. Leery admits her infidelity.

Joshua Jackson says Katie Holmes has never taken a bad picture in her life.

As the storm abates, steps are taken to restore the relationships that seemed so irreparable only hours earlier. Mr. Leery returns home and is ready to talk to his wife, who desperately wants to rebuild their marriage. Pacey and Tamara resume their affair. Dawson makes amends in both his relationship with Jen and his friendship with Joey.

ABOVE

Michelle Williams and Joshua Jackson take a break and share a laugh between scenes while shooting the show in Wilmington, North Carolina.

OPPOSITE

James Van Der Beek is Dawson Leery. James got his start in the 1995 movie *Angus* and he appeared in the little-seen movie *I Love You, I Love You Not,* with Claire Danes.

EPISODE
6
"LOOK WHO'S TALKING"

Pacey and Dawson go into the men's room at school to talk about Pacey's romance with his teacher. They thought it was safe to talk since there seemed to be no one else in the bathroom, but they couldn't see that there was another student in one of the stalls. By noon, just about everyone at Capeside High has heard about Pacey and Tamara.

Bessie goes into labor and Joey feebly tries to help her. When the ambulance can't get there in time, the two of them have to take a rowboat over to Dawson's house. As the birth gets closer and closer, they realize the only person they can now get to help Bessie give birth is Jen's grandmother.

Suddenly it looks like Bessie is in trouble because she seems to be losing a lot of blood. Dawson is filming the birth and Joey runs out of the room when she begins to panic. Finally, after some encouragement, Joey returns to the room to hold Bessie's hand through the difficult birth. Bessie has a healthy baby boy.

By the time the baby is born, just about everyone in town knows about Pacey and Tamara's affair. Eventually the two are called in front of the school board to confront the issue head on. Before all the accusations can fly, Pacey says the whole thing was a teenage fantasy and it didn't really happen. Tamara's career is saved, but later that night she tells Pacey that it is over and she's leaving town.

Joshua and James were actually roommates during the first season's filming.

"People called us the Odd Couple," says Joshua, "and I was definitely not Felix."

EPISODE

7

"THE BREAKFAST CLUB"

Dawson stumbles upon Pacey and Jen, seemingly in the middle of a joke. Pacey has just revealed that Dawson's childhood nickname was "Oompa Loompa." When Dawson asks what they are talking about, Jen doesn't tell him anything. Dawson later tricks Pacey in the locker room, saying that Jen told him about the conversation. When Pacey tells him that Oompa Loompa isn't such a terrible nickname, Dawson explodes at him.

Joey, meanwhile, is in another classroom giving an oral report on how six hundred women were once kept for the emperor during one of the Chinese dynasties. A guy who thinks he is the sexiest guy in school starts to make cracks, and then later he attempts to cut in front of Joey in the lunch line. By then she's had enough and she hits him. Detention for Joey!

Jen has a heated argument with a teacher and says, "Life is a bitch." Detention for Jen!

According to Michelle Williams, the cast "goes out to dinner occasionally and hangs out as a group. But when you work with people five or six days a week, that's plenty. I love them all to death, but I need a little time to myself!"

Dawson and Pacey get into a fight on the basketball court when Pacey makes the dreaded "Oompa" remark and Dawson throws a basketball in his face. Detention for Dawson!

When the three show up for Saturday morning detention, Pacey is there too but refuses to tell the group why. Abby, the school gossip, walks in and declares she is there for having an orgy in the boys' locker room.

The librarian leaves the room and the group starts wandering the halls and playing truth or dare. Pacey kisses Jen and Joey kisses Dawson during the game.

The girls stand around and watch the boys play basketball. If Dawson wins, Pacey has to reveal why he's been sent there for the day.

When Joey starts to make cutting remarks about Jen, Jen has finally had enough and asks Joey why she hates her so much. Abby says that it's very simple—they are both in love with the same guy.

Just as Abby shouts that the librarian is returning and they need to get back in a hurry, Dawson makes the winning shot. But the librarian has seen them, and makes them reorganize the card catalogs. During that time, Abby reveals that she really isn't the class slut but has had to show up because she's been tardy so many times.

Pacey finally reveals the reason he's in detention. After Dawson hit him with the basketball, the cheerleaders hugged and comforted him. He got so excited that he went into the boys' locker room to relieve himself and the coach walked in.

At the end of the day, Dawson tells Jen that he hates his nickname because it reveals that he's not an athletic kind of guy. Jen says it just doesn't matter because she loves him anyway.

In the last moments of detention, a tearful Joey says that she has found the right person, but if she tells him, everything would change between them.

Michelle and James looking beautiful. "I think James is going to be a huge star,"
says Kevin Williamson. "He's very serious and single-minded about acting. But
what's nice about him and the other kids is that they're unaffected. They're not yet
stars, so they're not concerned with the size of their trailer . . . yet!"

EPISODE

8

"ESCAPE FROM NEW YORK"

Dawson is at home when Joey stops by and says she can't get any sleep at her house with baby Alexander crying all the time. She spends the night with Dawson.

On the way to school, Pacey is complaining how dull the town is when a car comes speeding by and almost hits him. When the car stops, the driver asks where Capeside High is and then speeds off again.

When Jen, Joey, and Dawson begin to head off for their first class, Jen sees that the driver of the car is her ex-boyfriend Billy from New York. She ditches school to go see him. Later, when someone asks Dawson if Jen has another boyfriend, he runs to find Jen and Billy.

Billy needs a place to spend the night and Dawson offers, even though it's clear that he hates the guy. Billy is baiting Dawson, asking him what he wants to know about Jen. But Dawson doesn't bite, saying he knows everything he needs to know.

At the video store, Joey asks Pacey for a copy of *The English Patient*, saying that it's the only thing that will put the baby to sleep. Pacey tries to get Joey to admit that she's in love with Dawson, but she won't.

After spending the day with Billy, Jen says good-bye and we think he's on his way back to New York. But he shows up at a party later that night and tells Jen he needs another good-bye kiss. A furious

Dawson was comfortable with Joey crashing in his bed anytime she felt like it, until they went to visit her dad in jail and had to stay overnight in a motel. Suddenly, he began to have feelings toward her when they were lying together in an unfamiliar bed.

Dawson declares that one of them has got to go. Instead of making a choice between the two guys, Jen says that she's the one who's leaving.

Meanwhile Joey has been ditched—first by Pacey, who walked away to hit on other girls, and then by Dawson, who was going to get her a drink and then never returned after he spotted Jen. She is getting drunk and about to start making out with a handsome guy who is making advances toward her when Pacey comes to her aid.

Dawson and Pacey take Joey home and while Pacey is trying to put the baby to sleep with tales of *The English Patient,* Dawson is tucking a grateful Joey in bed. She leans up and kisses him. Later in the boat ride back across the creek, Dawson tells Pacey what happened. Pacey says that it's clear Joey is in love with Dawson.

Dawson watches Billy finally drive away and goes to talk with Jen on the pier the next day. To his surprise, Jen breaks up with him, saying she has to live her own life.

Jen tells Dawson that she needs time to herself. By the time she realizes that she really wants him, it's too late.

EPISODE 9
"IN THE COMPANY OF MEN"

Dawson is still pining for Jen when Billy returns to town. When Jen tells Billy to get lost, he goes looking for Dawson. Billy convinces Dawson and Pacey to go on a road trip with him to Providence so that Dawson can forget about Jen. When Jen asks where they are going, Billy lies and says he's taking them to a whorehouse.

Joey is walking to school when football team jock Warren pulls up to give her a ride. In the car he tries to convince Joey to have sex with him. She refuses, but later finds out from Jen that Warren has told the whole school they slept together. When Joey tries to confront Warren about what he said, Warren starts yelling at her loudly—so everyone can hear—that he would never be her boyfriend.

Joey runs out of school and Jen follows. Together they plot how they will get revenge. Eventually Joey talks to gossipy Abby about Warren and makes up a story about how they didn't use protection and now she is pregnant and Warren won't help her out. On cue, Abby tells everyone. When Warren comes back to his locker, he sees bumper stickers and baby dolls.

Abby later discovers that the story can't be true because she spoke to Warren's last girlfriend, who said he was unable to have sex. Joey is delighted and goes to talk to Warren. Out of fear that Joey will tell everyone about his problem, Warren tells everyone in sight that he didn't really sleep with Joey.

On a ferry to the island, Dawson, Pacey, and Billy decide to teach a bunch of wiseguys on the boat a lesson. Dawson attaches a hook to their car and Pacey moons them when they start to drive away.

When the other guys get furious and try to chase after them, their car snaps backward, pulling the rear tires off the car.

Later, at a club, Dawson meets a new girl and she's a film buff like he is. They have a great time together and eventually he kisses her goodnight.

At home, Joey and Jen are having a frank talk about guys. Jen says that Dawson is really in love with her and that she (Jen) is just a temporary fling. Later that night Joey goes over to talk to Dawson about what Jen has said. But Dawson is exhausted from his wild antics. He asks Joey if the conversation can wait—it will have to.

Katie says James and Joshua like teasing her off camera. "They always say things to get a rise out of me," she says. "They like to moon me!"

EPISODE 10
"MODERN ROMANCE"

Dawson and Jen decide they can still be friends, but the new friendship is put to the test when Jen tells him she's going out on a date with Cliff. Dawson quickly says that he has a date and asks if she wants to double. He scrambles to make a date with Mary Beth so he can go along.

In biology class, Pacey is the only student failing, so he agrees to do an extra-credit project studying snails with another student. He later finds out that the other student is Joey. It becomes a test of wills when the two of them try to work together.

Katie Holmes admits that she's a lot like Joey. "I'm kind of a tomboy," she says. "I think Joey and I react similarly to things like boys—the insecurities. Joey doesn't tell you how she's feeling. She holds it all in."

Disaster strikes when Pacey tries to get the snails to breed by putting a male in with the females. The male eats the females and Joey and Pacey are left without a science experiment.

Later that night, Dawson, Mary Beth, Jen, and Cliff are at the carnival together. The tension mounts when Dawson challenges Cliff to a game. Dawson desperately wants to win and when he does, he accidentally starts to hand his prize to Jen. Mary Beth is hurt and runs off. When Dawson finds her to apologize, Mary Beth admits that she has a crush on Cliff and Dawson admits that he still cares about Jen.

When they go back to the carnival, Dawson grabs Jen at the line for the Ferris wheel and Mary Beth grabs Cliff. Wouldn't it be fun if they traded partners for the ride? Once they are airborne, Dawson tells Jen that he still cares for her and doesn't understand why she dumped him. By this time, Jen is angry and confused.

Pacey and Joey, meanwhile, go to the local river to catch more snails. When they return to the boat, it has vanished, so they have to swim the icy river to make their way back to Pacey's truck. When they arrive, Pacey says they have to take off their clothes and wrap themselves in warm blankets. He leaves Joey alone to undress, but is secretly watching in the rearview mirror. Finally dried off, the two arrive at the carnival. Pacey asks if Dawson would mind if he asked Joey out. Dawson says yes, then no, and then finally yes again.

Later that night Pacey drops Joey off at home and tries to kiss her. When she doesn't respond, he realizes that their romance was not meant to be and that they should return to being pals.

Dawson goes to the video store the next day to tell Pacey that he doesn't want him to kiss Joey. Pacey says it's too late and makes up a story about a big romance. At first Dawson isn't sure what to believe, but finally Pacey admits that he made it up and tells Dawson that it's time for him to decide. Is it going to be the blonde or the brunette?

When Dawson finds out that Jen is going to the carnival with another date, he suddenly invites another girl and suggests that they go on a double date. But by the end of the evening he manages to get Jen alone for a heart-to-heart talk.

EPISODE
11
"FRIDAY THE 13TH"

This episode is a nod to the movies that made Kevin Williamson a famous name in Hollywood—*Scream* and *I Know What You Did Last Summer.*

In honor of Friday the 13th, Dawson plans a séance for his friends. They are already pretty shaky because there are reports that a serial killer is on the loose in Capeside. Then Jen gets an anonymous note and a creepy phone call and now everyone is freaked out.

When Pacey and Dawson make a run to the convenience store to get some snacks for the party, they see a girl who is being abused by her boyfriend. The guys rescue her and invite her to Dawson's.

At the séance, the kids begin to fear for their lives when the power suddenly goes out and Pacey spots a mysterious figure lurking outside the Leery house. Later, it turns out that the girl's boyfriend has been stalking them all along.

Dawson's Creek creator Kevin Williamson drew from his own teenage years to create the show. While growing up, Kevin, like Dawson, was obsessed with wanting to be like Steven Spielberg; he knew every line from Jaws by heart.

"This is sort of my childhood come to life in a lot of ways," says *Dawson* creator
Kevin Williamson. "That's why I'm so passionate about it and so involved with it.
I just want to create interesting relationships and interesting conversations."

EPISODE
12
"PRETTY WOMAN"

Capeside is holding a beauty contest and guess which familiar faces are contestants.

Joey decides to enter, and in a bid for the men's liberation movement so does Pacey. But in truth he does it mainly to impress the girls.

Joey has to sing in the competition and she needs a whole new look, so she turns to Jen for some help. The makeover impresses everyone—especially Dawson, who suddenly realizes what a beauty she is. Now he's really torn. Does he want Jen or Joey?

After seeing that Dawson is attracted to the new and improved Joey, Jen is beside herself with jealousy. And the green-eyed monster really rears its ugly head when Joey is the first-place runner-up.

Katie says her lawyer dad and homemaker mom don't get very upset when she utters some of the show's eyebrow-raising lines as Joey. "They just kind of laugh," she says.

EPISODE
13
SEASON FINALE
"BREAKING AWAY"

Joey has been offered an opportunity to spend next semester in France. She has two days to make her decision. Jen, who has renewed feelings for Dawson, is anxious to see Joey go away for a while.

Meanwhile, Joey learns that this year it is her turn to visit her father in prison for his birthday. Joey reluctantly decides to go and convinces Dawson to come along. They arrive too late at night to get in for a visit and realize they will have to stick around until the morning. They find a local motel in which to spend the night, but Dawson suddenly balks when it looks like they will have to sleep in the same bed together. Joey reassures him that they have slept in the same bed together for years.

The next day Dawson and Joey sit down for a visit with her dad. Things do not go smoothly and Joey blows up at her father and leaves abruptly. As Dawson gets up to follow her, Mr. Potter asks him to stay and tell him some things about his daughter. As he proceeds to talk about Joey's great qualities, Dawson suddenly realizes how strong his feelings are for her.

When Dawson meets up with Joey again, he asks her if she is really going to France. When she asks him for one good reason why she should stay, he is silent. "I thought so," says Joey.

Meanwhile, Jen finds out that her grandfather has had another stroke. She turns to Dawson for comfort and asks if she can spend the night with him.

The next morning Joey drops by and finds Dawson and Jen together. Joey runs off and Dawson goes after her. He tries to explain that there is nothing between him and Jen. Joey asks if Dawson is ready for honesty, because honesty changes everything. Dawson doesn't answer and Joey turns to leave. Dawson rushes up to her and kisses her.

It certainly *looked* like Joey was the object of Dawson's affection at the end of the first season.

THE SECOND SEASON

The gang of four is back in Capeside and it looks like the second season of *Dawson's Creek* is just as action-packed as the first. Here are just a few of the developments to rock the world of *Dawson's Creek* during season two:

Nothing Ever Stays the Same

The romance we've all been waiting for—Joey and Dawson, a couple at last. But the path of romance is never smooth. The long-time pals quickly discover that romantic involvement creates complications even between two people who have known each other for most of their lives. Relationship woes are no less complicated for Dawson's parents, who explore first an open relationship and then a trial separation.

Jen is freaking out about the budding romance between Dawson and Joey. Back in Capeside after a stint in New York, it seems she is back to her old wild ways, dating every guy in town. But it doesn't take long for her to realize that she is setting herself up for a big disappointment.

New Kids on the Block

Two new characters shake things up: Andie and Jack McPhee. Jack is played by Kerr Smith, who is best known for his role on *As the World Turns*. Andie is played by actress Meredith Monroe, best known from the television show *Dangerous Minds*.

Joey meets quiet and reserved Jack at the Ice House. An unforgettable kiss shakes up her already rocky relationship with Dawson, who is preoccupied with the turmoil in his parents' marriage.

Andie meets Pacey when she smacks into his car, but tries to make it up to him by getting him a date with a cheerleader. But it's Andie who is holding Pacey's undivided attention.

Joey meets Laura, an interior designer, who becomes both a mentor and a friend. She encourages Joey to develop her talent for the arts and draws out a side of her that is yet unexplored.

Are there vampires in Capeside? *Buffy the Vampire Slayer* star Sara Michelle Gellar makes a special guest appearance on *Dawson's Creek.*

Jen and Dawson . . . will they ever get back together?

THE CAST AND CREW
First air date: 1/20/98

PRODUCTION COMPANY
Columbia Tristar Television

EXECUTIVE PRODUCERS

Kevin Williamson   Paul Stupin

Charles Rosin   Deborah Joy Levine

DIRECTORS

Lou Antonio   Allan Arkush

Michael Fields   Steve Miner   Michael Uno

CAST

James Van Der Beek	Dawson Leery	Ian Bohen	Anderson Crawford
Michelle Williams	Jennifer Lindley	Dorothy R. Brown	Caroline Fields
Joshua Jackson	Pacey Witter	Linda Bureau	cheerleader
Katie Holmes	Josephine "Joey" Potter	Josh Crouch	smoker
Mary Margaret Humes	Gail Leery	Scott Foley	Cliff
John Wesley Shipp	Mitchell Leery	George Gaffney	Bodie
Mary Beth Pie	Grams	Ed Grady	Grandpa
Nina Repeta	Bessie Potter	Adrienne Harvey	cheerleader
Eion Bailey	Billy	Leann Hunley	Tamara Jacobs
Helen Baldwin	Mrs. Triangle	Monica Keena	Abby Morgan
Barry Bell	Coach	Travis Stanberry	Carl
Chris Berry	Eric		

SET

Even though the setting of *Dawson's Creek* is supposed to be Capeside, Massachusetts, a suburb of Boston, the show is actually shot at the Screen Gems Studios in Wilmington, North Carolina.

CREATED BY

The show's creator, Kevin Williamson, says the show is full of bits and pieces from his own life as a teenager growing up in New Bern, North Carolina. Just as Dawson dreams of one day doing, Kevin studied theater and film at East Carolina University before moving to New York City to start an acting career. He eventually moved to Los Angeles, where he tried his hand at writing and directing. His first real script was turned into the mega-hit film *Scream*.

Kevin says he really became a writer out of fear. "Fear is the greatest motivator," he says. "Fear of not being able to pay your bills and having the phone cut off. Those were the fears that pushed me to write *Scream*."

Kevin also used soundtracks to help him keep working. "I love soundtracks," he says. "When I was writing *Scream*, I listened to *Halloween* soundtracks, *Dressed to Kill*, and my favorite,. . . *Don't Look Now*. I actually write scenes around songs."

Kevin followed *Scream* with *I Know What You Did Last Summer*, which earned an amazing $70 million at the box office. Based on those success stories, Kevin was able to get the go-ahead to make *Dawson's Creek*. He likes to describe the show as *The Breakfast Club* meets *Invasion of the Body Snatchers*.

Young stars of the WB: the *Dawson's Creek* gang teams up with members of the cast of *Buffy the Vampire Slayer* for a photo op.

"This show is sort of my childhood come to life in a lot of ways," he says.

"That's why I'm so passionate about it and so involved with it. I just want to create interesting relationships and interesting conversations."

WANT TO WRITE TO THE CAST AND CREW?

Send your letters to:
Dawson's Creek
Warner Bros. Television Network
4000 Warner Boulevard
Burbank, CA 91522

The Official *Dawson's Creek* Web Site

www.dawsons-creek.com

BIBLIOGRAPHY

Catalano, Grace. Meet the stars of *Dawson's Creek*. New York: Bantam Doubleday Dell, 1998.

Dunn, Jancee. "TV Ingenue." *Rolling Stone*, September 17, 1998, pp. 44–48.

Epstein, Jeffrey. "Everything You Always Wanted to Know (and Then Some) about *Dawson's Creek*." *Soap Opera News*, February 10, 1998, pp. 30–33.

Fretts, Bruce. "High School Confidential." *Entertainment Weekly*, January 9, 1998, pp. 34–39.

Graham, Jennifer. "Dawson's Peak." *Teen People*, September 1998, pp. 68–73.

"Here's the Scoop." *Soap Opera Update*, March 3, 1998, pp. 38–39.

Johnson, Ted. "Dawson's Peak." *TV Guide*, March 7, 1998, pp. 20–25.

Lipton, Michael. "Creek God." *People*, March 23, 1998, pp. 77–78.

Lowry, Brian. "Teens Flow to Creek." *Los Angeles Times*, March 3 1998, p. F10.

Lubenski, Cathy. "Angst Runs Deep in *Dawson's Creek*." *New York Daily News: New York Vue*, April 11, 1998, pp. 6–8.

Mannarino, Melanie. "Dawson's Dirt." *Seventeen*, April 1998, p. 120.

Weeks, Janet. "The Gang of Four." *Boston Herald*, January 26, 1998, p. 34.